May this book inspire you to organize, collaborate, and succeed effortlessly in your personal and professional life.

This one is for you!

TABLE OF CONTENTS

INTRODUCTION

This book is a game-changer! You will soon find out.

In today's fast-paced digital world, staying organized is not just a luxury—it's a necessity. Whether you're managing work documents, personal photos, or collaborative projects, the ability to access your files quickly and securely across devices can save you time, reduce stress, and boost productivity. That's where Microsoft OneDrive steps in, offering a reliable and powerful cloud storage solution that fits seamlessly into both your professional and personal life.

Welcome to *Microsoft OneDrive Success Guide*! This book is your ultimate guide to mastering the art of cloud storage, file management, and collaboration with OneDrive. No matter your level of experience—whether you're a complete beginner, a tech-savvy professional, or someone trying to learn the ropes—this guide is designed to equip you with the tools and knowledge to make OneDrive work for you.

Imagine being able to:

- Access your files anytime, anywhere, on any device.
- Share important documents with a single click, while maintaining full control over who can view or edit them.

- Collaborate in real-time on projects, without worrying about version conflicts or lost changes.
- Keep your digital life secure with state-of-the-art protection features.
- Integrate OneDrive with other Microsoft apps for a smooth, interconnected experience.

That's the magic of Microsoft OneDrive.

Why This Book?

Microsoft OneDrive is packed with features, but it can feel overwhelming to figure out where to start. Many users stick to the basics, missing out on the full range of tools that could make their lives easier. This book is here to change that. You'll find all the essential information you need right here, organized in a way that's simple, actionable, and enjoyable to follow.

Each chapter breaks down a key aspect of OneDrive, from setting up your account to troubleshooting common issues. Along the way, you'll find practical tips, real-world examples, and insider tricks that go beyond the basics.

The Power of Cloud Storage

With OneDrive, your files are stored safely in the cloud, giving you the flexibility to access them from anywhere while keeping your local devices clutter-free.

Beyond convenience, OneDrive opens the door to collaboration like never before. Need to share a presentation with a colleague? Done. Want to organize your family vacation photos and share them with relatives? Easy. With OneDrive, the possibilities are endless, and this book will show you how to unlock them all.

Your Journey Starts Here

If you've ever felt overwhelmed by the sheer volume of digital files you manage daily, or if you've hesitated to explore cloud storage because it seemed too complex, this book will be a game-changer. With *Microsoft OneDrive Success Guide*, you'll gain the confidence to not only manage your files effectively but also embrace a simpler, more organized way of working and living.

CHAPTER ONE

WELCOME TO ONEDRIVE

You are welcome to OneDrive. This book will help you establish a solid foundation that will help you make the most of Microsoft's versatile cloud storage service. No matter what your goal is, this book will guide you through the essential first steps. You will be better able to securely back up your files, collaborate on professional documents, or gain a better understanding of cloud storage solutions. Surely, at the end of this chapter, you will be navigating OneDrive with confidence, and maximizing its features to enhance productivity and organization.

Setting Up Your OneDrive Account

Before you can use OneDrive's features, you will need to open/have a Microsoft account. If you are already a user of Microsoft services—like Outlook, or Windows—all you have to do is log in using your existing credentials. If you are new to Microsoft, let us go through the steps to help you create an account. With the account, you will be ready to access everything that OneDrive has to offer.

How to Create a Microsoft Account

Follow these straightforward steps to set up a Microsoft account:

1. Go to the **Microsoft Account Sign-Up Page** at **https://signup.live.com/?lic=1**. Start your registration.

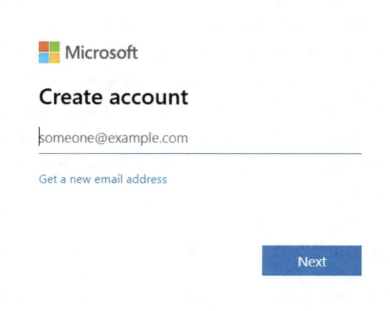

2. Enter your information—Provide basic details like your email address, password, and personal information, such as your name and date of birth. If you don't have an email, it's not an issue--you can create a free Outlook.com email account on this same page.

3. Microsoft will request identity verification. It will be sent through a code to your email or phone. This will help secure your account from unauthorized access.

4. Follow the prompts on your screen to complete the sign-up process. Once you are done, your Microsoft account will be ready for use.

Getting Started With OneDrive

Since you now have a Microsoft account, accessing OneDrive becomes very easy. Here is how to get started:

1. Navigate to the OneDrive website **Microsoft Account** at onedrive.live.com and sign in with your Microsoft credentials to access your OneDrive dashboard.

 Microsoft

Sign in

Email, phone, or Skype

No account? Create one!

Next

🔑 Sign-in options

2. Once you have logged in, familiarize yourself with the interface. There are main sections that are designed to help you organize and manage your files:

- Files: The primary storage area where all your uploaded and synced files appear. From here, you can create folders, upload new documents, and organize everything in one place.

- Recent: In this section, your recently accessed files are displayed. It makes it easy for you to pick up where you left off on any project.

- Shared: In this section, you'll find documents and folders that others have shared with you, as well as files you've shared with others. You will learn about sharing and collaboration in a subsequent chapter.

- Recycle Bin: this is where deleted files are stored temporarily. This section allows you the chance to recover any mistakenly removed documents. You can either restore these files or permanently delete them.

When you have completed these steps above, you're well on your way to becoming a confident OneDrive user, ready to explore the endless possibilities of cloud storage and collaboration.

Navigating the OneDrive Interface

Let's get you familiar with the layout, features, and functions of the OneDrive interface.

The Navigation Pane

This is found on the left side of the screen, this pane gives you quick access to critical areas such as:

- Files: your main workspace where all uploaded and synced files are stored.
- Photos: this is a dedicated section for organizing and viewing your images.
- Recycle Bin: A temporary storage for deleted files, allowing you to recover items or permanently delete them.
- Shared Items: This is where files and folders you've shared with others or that others have shared with you are displayed.

File List

This is the main section on the interface. It displays your files and folders. Here, you can upload, create, organize, and manage all your content, from personal documents to collaborative work files.

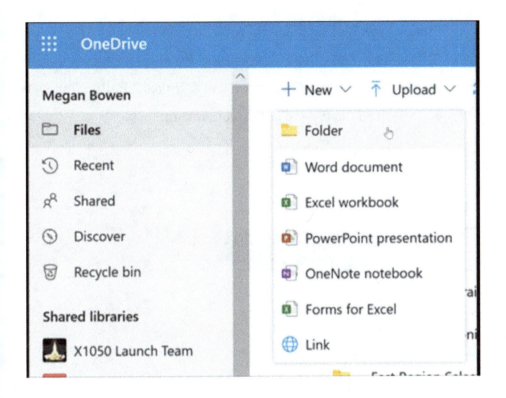

Key Features of OneDrive

In OneDrive, you have a variety of features that help you manage your files properly.

- Upload Files: To add files or folders from your device, simply click the "New & Upload" button on the command bar. You can upload everything from photos to project files, ensuring they're accessible from any connected device.

- Create New Files or Folders: You can create folders or even new Office files (like Word documents, Excel sheets, etc.) directly within the platform. Click the "New & Upload" button and select your desired file type to get started instantly.

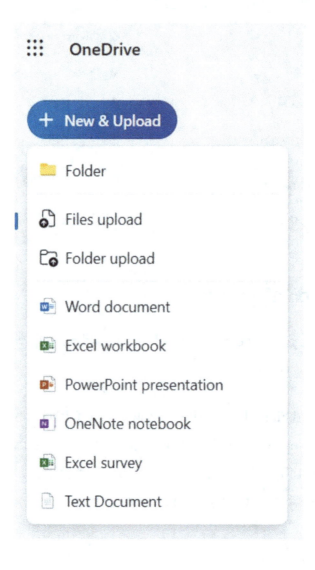

- Search Functionality: There is a **search bar** at the top to locate specific files or folders in seconds. This feature is very helpful if you have a large collection of documents and need to find something quickly.
- Sharing: Collaboration is fast and easy in OneDrive. Simply click the "Share" button next to any file to generate a shareable link or directly invite others to view or edit the file.

Free vs Paid OneDrive Plans

There is a range of plans that OneDrive offers to accommodate different storage needs and feature preferences. You need to understand the difference between free and paid options to be able to make an informed choice that suits you best.

Free Plan

- Storage Limit: The free plan provides **5 GB** of storage. This is enough for you to store essential documents, photos, and small collections of personal files.
- Basic Features: You can upload, share, and sync files across devices. It gives you a straightforward cloud storage experience without additional costs.

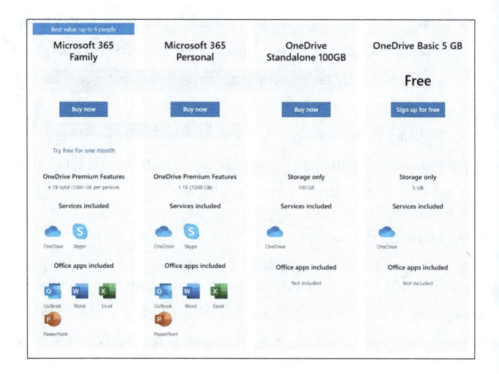

Paid Plans

- Microsoft 365 Personal: This plan offers **1 TB** of storage along with advanced security options and access to premium Microsoft Office applications (Word, Excel, PowerPoint, and more). It is ideal for individuals who require extra storage and advanced features.

- Microsoft 365 Family: This was designed for households. This plan provides the same benefits as the Personal plan but offers access to up to six users. Each member of the family plan receives their own 1 TB of storage, making it an excellent choice for families.

- Standalone OneDrive Plans: In this plan, you can purchase additional OneDrive storage separately. This option is ideal if you don't need the full Microsoft 365 suite but require more space for your files.

Choosing the Right Plan

Check the types and amount of data you'll be storing, and whether you need access to Office applications. If you're primarily storing documents, the free plan may suffice because they don't use up so much space. However, for larger file collections or advanced productivity tools, a paid plan may be worth it.

Microsoft frequently offers discounts and promotions on their services. It's worth checking their website to see if there are any current deals on OneDrive or Microsoft 365 plans. They are usually worth it.

Benefits of Using OneDrive

OneDrive does more than just store files. It is a powerful tool that can simplify your digital life, enhance collaboration, and protect your information. Below are some practical benefits of using OneDrive:

1. Backs up your files securely: OneDrive is a reliable way to back up your essential files. Storing files in the cloud protects them against local hardware failures or accidental deletion. Imagine the peace of mind knowing that if your computer crashes or phone is misplaced, all your data remains safe and accessible from any device connected to the internet.

2. You can access files from anywhere and anytime: With OneDrive, your files go with you to wherever you go. Whether you're working from a computer, tablet, or smartphone, your documents are always easy to reach. Imagine you're traveling and urgently need to access a presentation. All you need to do is simply log in from any device, and it's there.

3. Seamless collaboration: With OneDrive, teamwork is simplified. It has sharing and real-time editing capabilities. Share documents with colleagues, friends, or family members and collaborate on them simultaneously. For instance, if you're part of a project team, everyone can edit the document in real time. Each change is instantly visible to all.

4. Keeps you organized: OneDrive helps you to organize your files effectively with folders, tags, and a powerful search function. You are able to quickly locate documents, photos, or presentations, so you can spend less time searching and more time achieving.

5. Efficient security features: With OneDrive, security is a top priority. Files are encrypted both during transfer and while

stored. This makes sure you have confidentiality and privacy. Other features like version history allow you to retrieve previous versions of a document in case of accidental edits. This adds another layer of protection.

6. Integrates seamlessly with Microsoft services: It integrates with Microsoft applications (like Word, Excel, and PowerPoint) making it easy to work directly on documents without constantly downloading or re-uploading files. You can, for instance, create a new Word or Excel document within OneDrive and start editing immediately through Microsoft Word or Excel Online.

CHAPTER TWO

UPLOADING AND STORING FILES

N ow that you have familiarized yourself with what OneDrive has to offer, let us explore two core tasks for mastering OneDrive: uploading files and organizing them effectively. By understanding these processes, you'll ensure that your files are securely stored in the cloud and organized in a way that makes them easy to find and manage.

Uploading Files to OneDrive

This is a basic skill that enables you to store and access your documents, photos, videos, and other critical files from any device. There are various methods you can choose from. Choose the one that works best for you. Let us consider the various methods and a step by step guide for all the methods:

Uploading Using the Desktop App

OneDrive uses a desktop app. It makes it even easier to upload files by syncing them directly from your computer's file explorer. Let us consider how to get started:

1. Install the OneDrive Desktop App: Start by downloading and installing the OneDrive app if you haven't already. Once you have installed it, open the app and sign in with your Microsoft account. It is very probable that you have the app pre-installed in your system already.

2. Sync Folders: Once you have signed in, you'll be prompted to choose folders on your computer that you want to sync with OneDrive. You can add or change these folders anytime from the app's settings.

3. Drag-and-Drop: To upload files, drag them into the designated OneDrive folder on your computer. The app will automatically sync these files to the OneDrive cloud.

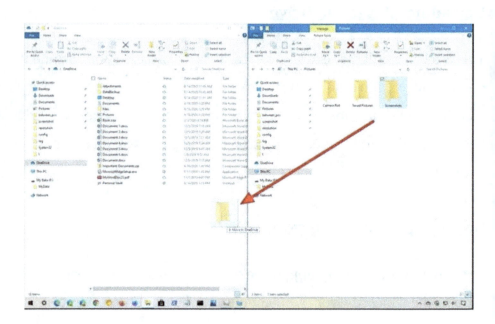

Uploading Using the Web Interface

1. Open your web browser. Go to the **OneDrive website**: https://onedrive.live.com. Log in with your **Microsoft account** (email and password). If you don't have an account, click on **Sign up** and create one. We dealt with that in Chapter One.

2. After logging in, you'll see your OneDrive home page. This is where all your files and folders are displayed. Decide where you want to upload your files: If you want them in a specific folder, click on the folder to open it. If you want them in the main directory, stay on the home page.

3. There are 2 options to do this:

   - First Option: Open the folder on your computer where the files are stored. Select the file(s) you want to upload. Drag the file(s) from your computer into the OneDrive browser window. Drop them into the area labeled **"Drag files here to upload"** or anywhere within the file list area.

   - Second option: Click the **Upload** button at the top of the page (near the toolbar). Select either: **Files** to upload individual files, or **Folder** to upload an entire folder. A file browser window will open. Navigate to the file or folder on your computer. Select the file or folder, then click **Open**.

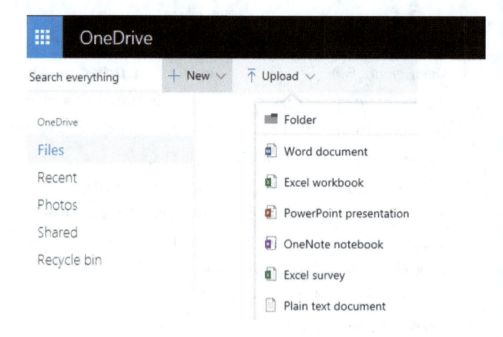

4. A progress indicator will appear, showing the upload status. Larger files may take longer, depending on your internet speed.

5. Once uploaded, the file(s) will appear in the chosen location in your OneDrive. You can check by: Looking for the file name in the list, or by confirming a green checkmark or uploaded status next to the file.

6. Rename files: Right-click the file > **Rename**. Move files: Right-click the file > **Move to** > Choose destination folder. Create folders: Click **New** > **Folder** > Name it > Click **Create**.

Uploading from Mobile Devices

The process of uploading files from mobile devices, such as smartphones and tablets, is also straightforward with the OneDrive mobile app:

1. Download the OneDrive App: Install the OneDrive app from the App Store (iOS) *apps.apple.com* or Google Play Store (Android) *play.google.com*.

2. Open the App and Sign In: Launch the app and sign in with your Microsoft account. Remember the account you opened in Chapter one?

3. Upload Files: Tap the **+** button or **Upload** option within the app. You can upload files from your device's storage or capture new photos and videos.

4. Select the files you want to upload, and the app will automatically upload them to your OneDrive storage.

 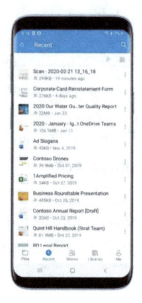 

Tips for Successful Uploads

- Make Sure You Have Stable Internet Connection: For smooth and uninterrupted uploads, a stable internet connection is necessary, especially when uploading large files.

- Be Aware of File Size Limits: OneDrive supports large files, but it's good to be mindful of file size limits, especially if uploading multiple large files at once.

- Organize as You Upload: It is faster and more efficient if you upload files directly into their intended folders. This practice will help keep your OneDrive account organized.

Organizing Your Files and Folders

Organizing your files is just as important as uploading them. By creating a clean, sensible structure, you can quickly locate files, saving time and reducing stress. The following are effective strategies for managing your OneDrive folders and files.

Create and Manage Folders

1. Creating a New Folder:
   - Through the Web Interface: In OneDrive, navigate to where you want the new folder. Click the **New** button on the command bar and select **Folder**. Enter a name and click **Create** to confirm.
   - Through the Desktop App: Open your OneDrive folder on your computer, right-click in the directory where you want a new folder, and select **New Folder**. Name it and press **Enter** to finalize.
2. Organizing Files into Folders:
   - Drag and Drop: To move files into folders, drag them from the file list and drop them into the appropriate folder.
   - Copy/Cut and Paste: You can right-click a file, select **Copy/Cut**, navigate to the target folder, right-click in the folder, and select **Paste**.
3. Renaming and Deleting Folders:

- To Rename: Right-click the folder you wish to rename, select **Rename**, and type the new name.
- To Delete: To delete a folder, right-click on it and select **Delete**. The folder will be moved to the Recycle Bin, where you can recover it if needed.

How to Use Tags and Descriptions

To have efficient organization, you will not only rely on folders. Learn to use descriptive file names and thoughtful folder structures to make your files even easier to locate. The following are a few tips:

- Descriptive Naming: Give your files clear and descriptive names. Instead of generic names like "Document1," or "File2," use a naming convention that includes details such as the year, project, or type (e.g., **2025_OspinaProject_Proposal**).
- Use Folder Hierarchy: Create a logical hierarchy for your folders. For instance, you might have a top-level folder named **Career** with subfolders for **Projects**, **Reports**, and **Presentations**. This structure can make browsing for specific files much easier.
- Use Tags and Keywords: OneDrive doesn't support tagging natively, but you can simulate it by using keywords in file and folder names. These keywords can be helpful when using the

search function to locate files with similar themes. That of course takes us back to descriptive naming.

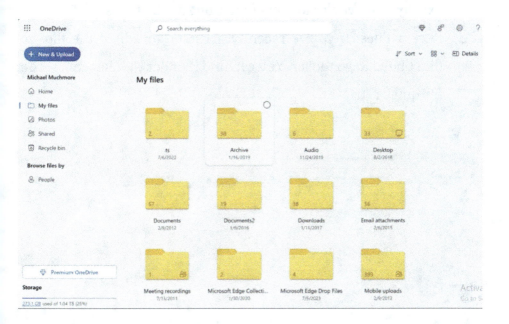

How to Use Search Function

The search feature in OneDrive is a powerful tool that allows you to quickly locate files and folders, even in a large collection. Here's how to use it effectively:

1. Search Bar: At the top of the OneDrive web interface, type in keywords related to the file or folder you're searching for. The search will pull up any file or folder that matches, saving you from manual browsing.

2. Filters: Refine your search results using filters like file type, date modified, or even specific keywords. This can help you pinpoint exactly what you're looking for among a sea of files.

3. Recent Files: If you've recently accessed or edited the file, you don't need to go too far. You can find it under the "Recent" section for quick retrieval.

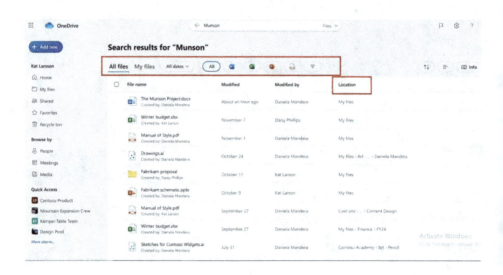

Tips for Effective File Management

- Carry out Regular Maintenance: Review and declutter your OneDrive periodically by removing outdated or unnecessary files to free up space and enhance organization.

- Backup Important Files: Regularly back up critical files to another storage location as an added layer of protection against data loss.

- Use Version History: If you need to revert to an earlier version of a file, OneDrive's version history feature is invaluable. Right-click on the file, select "Version History," and restore the desired version.

Managing different File Types and Size

You can store various file types and sizes in OneDrive, from documents to high-resolution videos. Here's how to manage different types of files effectively:

Document Files

- Uploading: You can upload documents like Word files, PDFs, and Excel spreadsheets using the methods discussed earlier.
- Viewing and Editing: You can view and edit many document types directly in OneDrive. For instance, Microsoft Office files can be opened and edited seamlessly using Office Online, preserving formatting and compatibility.

Photo and Video Files

- Uploading: You can upload photos and videos directly from your device's gallery or camera roll, either through the web or mobile apps.

- Organizing: Create a dedicated folder for photos and videos to keep them organized. Consider adding subfolders to categorize by events, dates, or themes (e.g., "Summer Vacation 2025" or "Wedding Party").

Large Files

- Handling Large Uploads: if the files you want to upload are very large files, ensure you have a stable internet connection to prevent interruptions. If a file fails to upload completely, OneDrive will attempt to resume from where it left off.
- Compression: If you encounter issues uploading large files, consider compressing them into a ZIP file before upload to reduce file size and potentially improve upload speed.

Unsupported File Types

- Check Compatibility: OneDrive supports most common file types, but certain specialized or proprietary formats may not be viewable or editable within the platform. Consult OneDrive's documentation for a complete list of supported file types.

Practical Scenarios for Uploading and Storing Files

Let us illustrate how OneDrive can be used for different needs effectively with the following scenarios:

Scenario 1: Backing Up Family Photos

Imagine you've taken a lot of photos over the past year and want to back them up to OneDrive to free up space on your phone.

1. **Create a Folder**: Begin by creating a folder named **"Family Photos"** in OneDrive.
2. **Upload Photos**: Use the mobile app to upload your photos directly from your phone's gallery to the "Family Photos" folder. Open the OneDrive app, go to your **Files** dashboard, tap the **+** sign at the top right, and select **Upload**. Then, navigate to your gallery, select the desired photos, and they will be uploaded to OneDrive.
3. **Organize by Event**: Within the "Family Photos" folder, create subfolders for different events, such as **"Wedding Reception 2025"** or **"Anne Birthday Party."** This will make it easier to locate specific memories later.

Scenario 2: Collaborating on a Work Project

If you are working with your team on a project and need to share documents and collaborate in real-time, OneDrive provides tools to streamline collaboration:

1. Upload Project Documents: Upload relevant documents into a folder you can title like this— **"Deforestation Project 2025."**
2. Share the Folder: Click **Share** on the folder and invite team members, assigning them editing permissions. (We'll discuss permissions in a later chapter.)
3. Collaborate in Real-Time: With Office Online, you and your teammates can edit documents simultaneously, leaving comments and making updates as needed.

Scenario 3: Managing School Assignments

Let us assume that you want to organize and access your school assignments from any device for convenient studying and submission:

1. Create Folders: Set up folders for each subject or semester, such as **"Math 101"** or **"History Semester 1."**
2. Upload Assignments: Save your assignments and notes in the appropriate subject folders.

3. Sync across Devices: Make sure your OneDrive is synced with your devices so you can access your work from anywhere, whether on your phone, laptop, or tablet. We will discuss syncing in the next chapter.

Scenario 4: Storing and Accessing Large Media Files

Suppose you've created a high-resolution video and need to store it securely in the cloud:

1. Create a Folder: In OneDrive, create a folder you can name something like **"Media Files"** for all your large media assets.
2. Upload the Video: Upload the video file. If the file is exceptionally large, check that your internet connection is stable to avoid interruptions.
3. Access from Anywhere: You can access the video from any device and share it with collaborators as needed, making it easy to manage large media files.

CHAPTER THREE

SYNCING ACROSS DEVICES

Syncing OneDrive across multiple devices is one of the most important uses of OneDrive. It is an essential feature for anyone wanting access to up-to-date files no matter where they are, and with whatever device that is available and convenient. This chapter will guide you through setting up and managing synchronization effectively on various platforms, from PCs to smartphones and tablets.

What is OneDrive Syncing?

With syncing, any change you make to files on one device automatically reflects on other connected devices. Here's a breakdown of how syncing works:

- Two-Way Synchronization: Updates on any device sync across all others, keeping everything current.
- Real-Time Updates: Save a file, make changes to the file, and OneDrive will sync those changes immediately, making the latest version accessible from any device.

- Local and Cloud Storage: Files are stored locally on your device and in the cloud, ensuring offline access as needed.

Syncing is beneficial to the user because it helps in consistency, accessibility, and convenience.

Setting Up OneDrive Sync on Windows

1. Launch OneDrive: Find it in the Start menu or system tray.

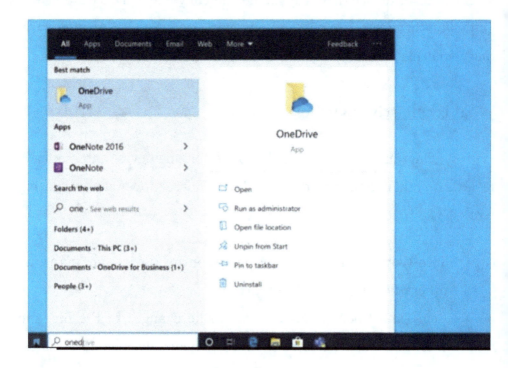

2. Sign In: Use your Microsoft account to sign in.

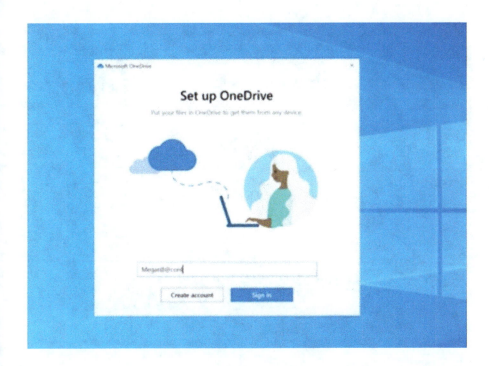

3. Finish setting up. Click on **open my One Drive** to see the syncing files.

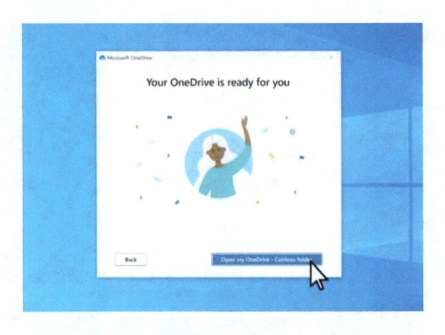

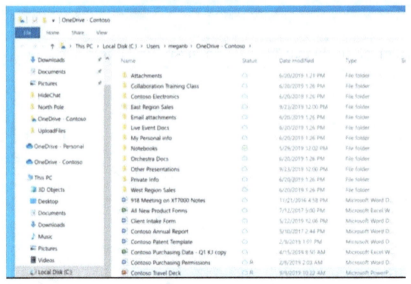

4. Drag and drop files from your computer to OneDrive.

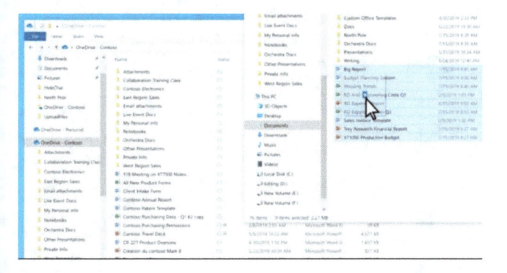

5. Complete Setup: Your OneDrive folder is ready for use in File Explorer.

Managing Sync Settings

- Selective Sync: Adjust folder syncing by right-clicking on the OneDrive icon in the taskbar of your computer, selecting "Settings," then choosing which folders to sync.
- Pause Syncing: Temporarily halt syncing if needed by selecting "Pause syncing" in the taskbar icon.
- Check Sync Status: Click on the icon in the taskbar of your desktop to view the sync status.

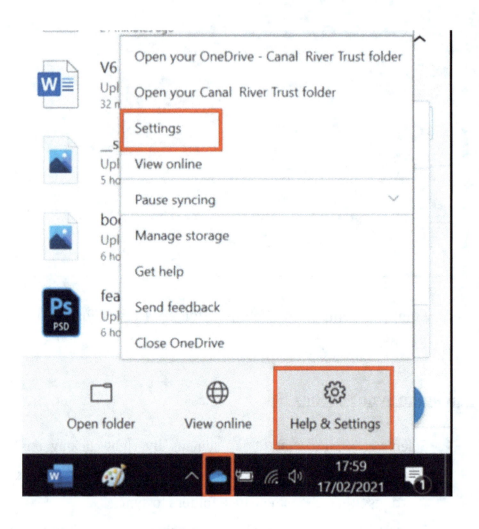

Syncing OneDrive on Mac OS

1. Download OneDrive: Visit Microsoft's OneDrive download page. I
   keep repeating this even though I'm sure by now you must have
   downloaded it.

2. Install and Open: Drag the OneDrive icon to the Applications folder and launch it.

3. Sign In: Enter your Microsoft account details.

4. Choose Folder Location: Decide where to save the OneDrive folder.

5. Select Folders to Sync: Select the folders you want to sync.

6. Finish Setup: The folder will appear in Finder for easy access.

Syncing OneDrive on Mobile Devices

- **On Apple Devices,**
- Install OneDrive from the Apple Store.
- Sign in using your Microsoft account.
- Set up sync so your files can automatically sync.
- Enable offline access by tapping on the ellipses on files and select **Make Available Offline**.
- **On Android Devices,**
- Install the OneDrive app from the Google Play Store.
- Sign in with your Microsoft account.
- Set up sync so the app will start syncing files.
- Enable offline access using the three-dot menu.

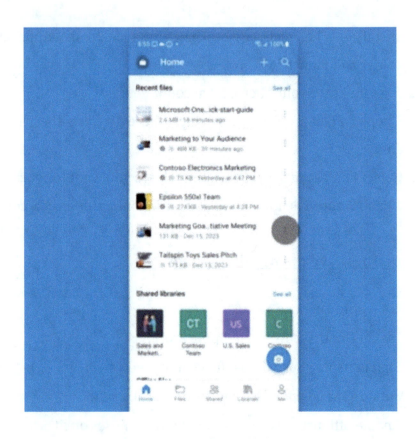

Tap the three dots to set up offline access

Toggle to the right the **Make available offline** option

Managing Sync Settings on Mobile

On iPhone,

- Auto-Upload Photos and Videos: Open OneDrive on your mobile. Select the Accounts icon. Select **Settings.** Select **Uploads**. Tap **Camera Upload**. Tap the gear button on the right side to auto-upload photos.

- Manage Storage: Monitor storage usage to avoid overloading OneDrive.

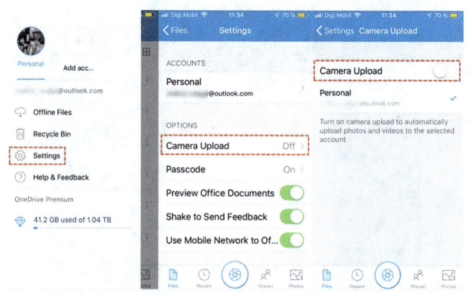

Turn on OneDrive Camera Upload on iPhone

On Android,

- Sign in and select the **Me** icon located at the upper left corner. Select **Settings**. Then select **Camera Upload**. Turn on the gear button beside it.

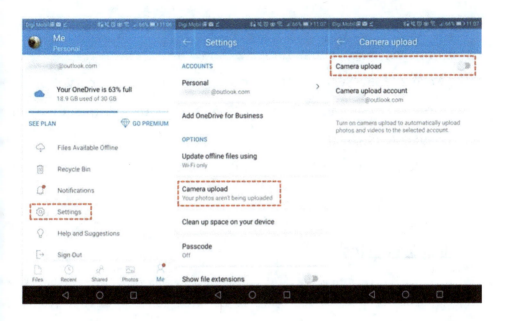

Tips for Effective Syncing

1. Always Keep Software Updated: Ensure both the OS and OneDrive app are current to improve performance.

2. Use Selective Sync: Select specific folders for each device to save storage space.

3. Monitor Sync Status: Regularly check for sync issues.

4. Resolve Conflicts: Handle "conflicted copy" files when multiple edits occur simultaneously. We will discuss on this much later in this book.

5. Offline Access: Make critical files available offline for easy access during travel.

6. Real-Time Collaboration: Syncing is great for collaborative projects; share folders for easy teamwork.

7. Secure Your Syncing: Use strong passwords and encryption to protect your data. We will discuss how to get this done in subsequent chapter.

8. Backup Important Files: Consider additional backups for crucial files.

Practical Scenarios

Scenario 1: Working Remotely

- Sync Files Before Leaving: Sync project files before leaving the office.
- Access at Home: Open synced files from your home device.
- Save Changes: Any edits made at home will automatically update on OneDrive.

Scenario 2: Traveling Without Internet

1. Enable Offline Access: Make key files available offline before you leave.

2. Files Sync When Connected: Once back online, any changes will automatically sync.

Scenario 3: Collaborative Project

- Share a Folder: Share project folders with the team. We will discuss how to share in a subsequent chapter.
- Collaborate in Real-Time: All updates will sync for everyone in the shared folder.

Scenario 4: Managing Multiple Devices

- Install OneDrive: Set it up on all your devices.
- Selectively Sync: Sync only necessary folders to each device.
- Access Anywhere: Edits on any device will sync across them all.

CHAPTER FOUR

SHARING FILES AND COLLABORATING

L et us discuss how to share files and collaborate effectively using OneDrive. Whether you're working on a team project, sharing photos, or collaborating on a document, OneDrive's sharing and collaboration features are designed to make teamwork efficient and secure.

Sharing Files and Folder

- Sharing via the Web Interface
    1. Go to the OneDrive website and sign in to your Microsoft account.
    2. Right-click the item you want to share and select "Share" from the menu. Or click on the share icon in front of the item.

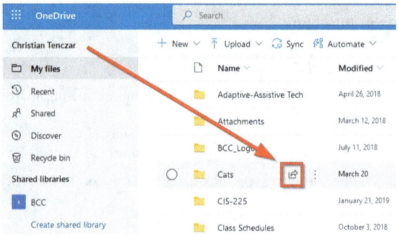

Using the share icon

3. In the dialog box that is shown, choose one of these options: **Anyone with the Link** will allow anyone with the

link to access the file. You can set permissions to allow editing or viewing. Choose **Specific People** to limit access to specific email addresses. They'll need to sign in to their Microsoft account or use a passcode.

4. Set permissions by choosing **Allow Editing** for collaborators, or disable it for view-only access. Add an optional message for the email notification.

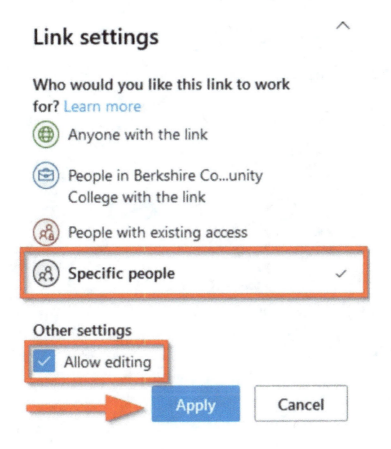

5. Click **Send** to email the link, or **Copy link** to paste it elsewhere. You can also choose to click on **Outlook**. It will give you the opportunity to write a custom note along the file.

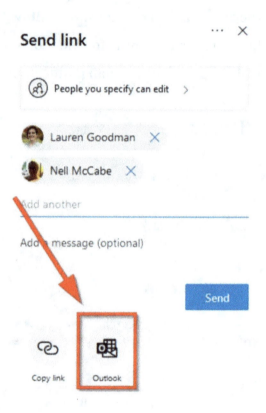

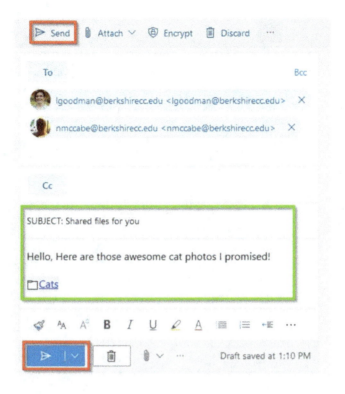

You can attach a custom message if you use outlook. But you can still send without using outlook and the receiver will receive a notification.

- Sharing via Desktop App
    1. Navigate to your OneDrive folder in File Explorer (Windows) or Finder (Mac).
    2. Right-click the file or folder, select Share, and configure settings like in the web interface above.
    3. Send via email or copy the link to share.

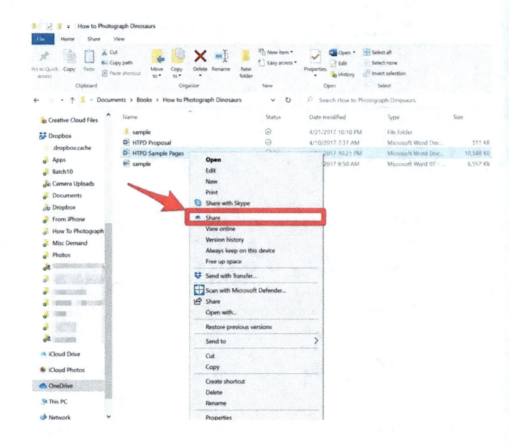

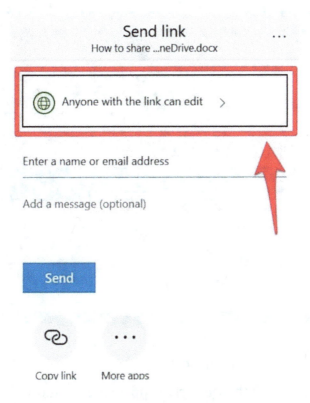

- Sharing Files by sharing a link: Open the **Send link** window. Click on **Copy**. Edit permissions and apply. Click on copy and paste on your emails.

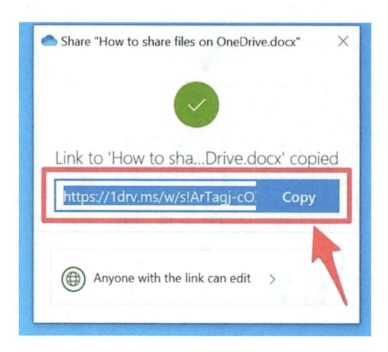

- Sharing via Mobile Devices
    1. Launch the OneDrive app on iOS or Android.
    2. Tap the ellipsis (three dots) next to the item, select **Share**, and choose sharing options.

When someone shares a file or folder with you, you will receive an email or notification on your device. To see files shared with you in your One Drive app, select the **Shared** view icon at the bottom of the app. This **Shared** view area contains files shared with you by others and files you shared with others.

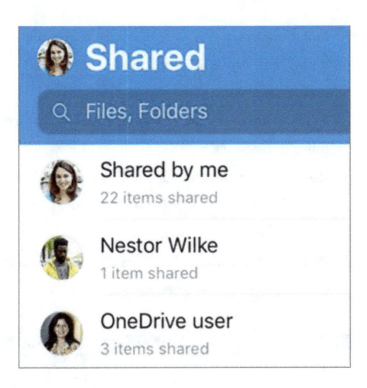

Tips for Effective Sharing

- Review permissions regularly to ensure only authorized individuals have access.
- Use expiration dates for time-limited access.
- Monitor activity to see who has viewed or edited files.

Collaborating on Documents

- Real-Time Co-Authoring

1. Collaborators are those you have shared your documents with. They can edit Word, Excel, or PowerPoint files in real-time.

2. Track changes by using the **Comments** feature to leave notes or feedback.

- Use Office Online for Collaboration

    1. Open Office from OneDrive online and edit the document directly from your browser.

    2. Invite additional collaborators by sharing access to the document from the **share** button.

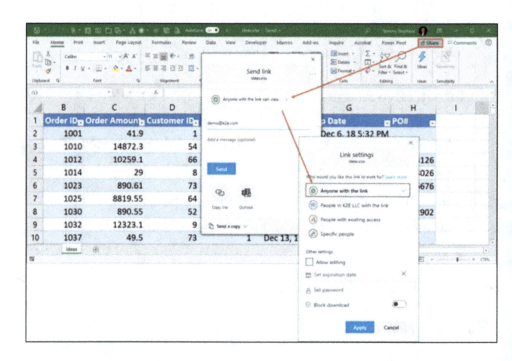

- Comments and Mentions
  1. Add comments to specific parts of the document that you need to. You can add comment by clicking the comment button near the window's upper right area. Alternatively, you can select the part of the document you want to comment on, right-click on your mouse, and select **New Comment** to comment. Once you comment, others can leave a reply.

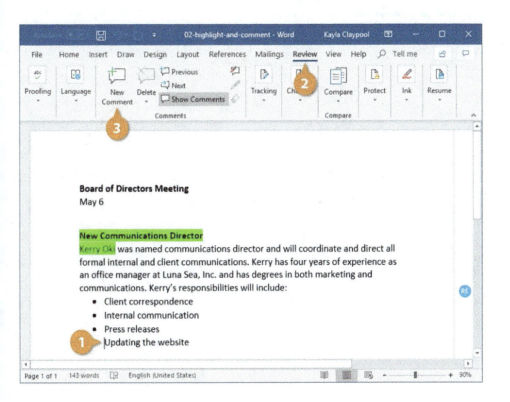

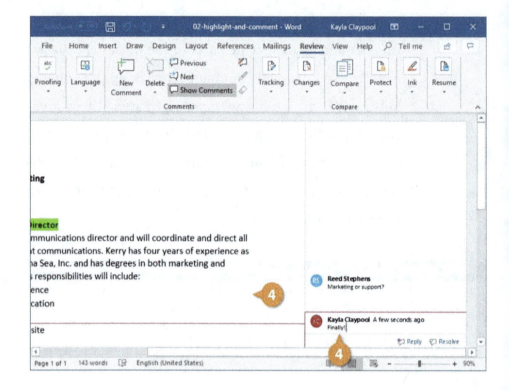

2. Using @Mentions, tag specific collaborators to draw their attention to the comments made.

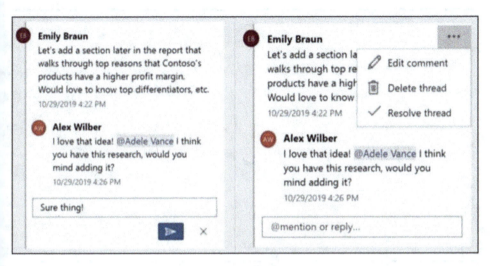

An example of threaded comments using mentions.

How to Manage Shared Files and Permissions

- To view sharing permissions, right-click the item and select **share** to see who has access to the file you shared, and to see files shared with you.

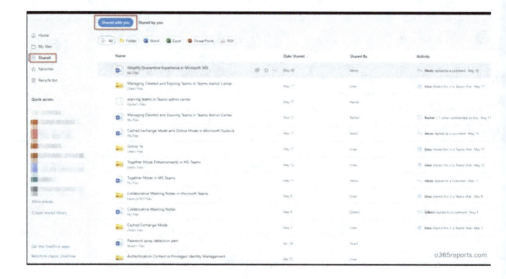

- Managing who can view or edit your files in OneDrive is simple. Follow the steps below to take control of access permissions:

  1. Open Your OneDrive Account
     Log into your OneDrive or SharePoint account and locate the **"My files"** or **"Documents"** section. This is where all your stored files and folders are organized.
  2. Locate the File or Folder
     Browse through your files and select the specific file or folder you want to manage. This could be a document, image, or any other type of file.
  3. Access the Options Menu
     Hover over the selected file or folder and click on the three-

dot menu (More) icon that appears beside it. This menu
contains various options for managing your file.

4. Select **"Manage Access"**

   From the dropdown menu, choose the **"Manage access"**
   option. This will direct you to a detailed settings page where
   you can view and adjust access permissions.

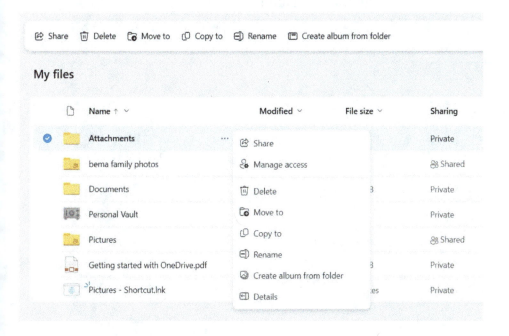

5. Review Current Permissions

   On the **"Manage Access"** page, you'll see a list of individuals
   or groups who have access to the file or folder. The list also
   shows their current permission level, such as **Can Edit** or
   Can View.

6. Adjust Access Permissions

- To modify someone's permissions, click the corresponding option next to their name.
- To remove access entirely, select the appropriate option to revoke their permissions.
- To add a new user, use the sharing link or the invite feature provided.

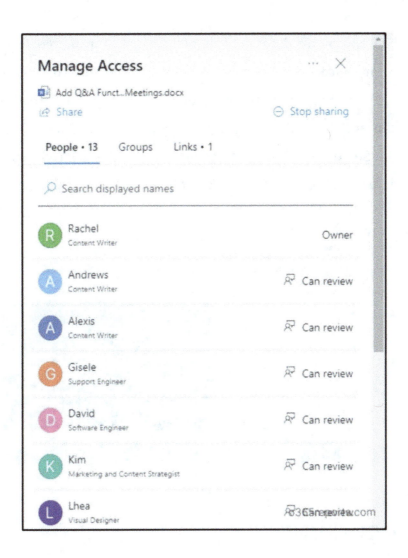

7. Save Your Changes

   Ensure that any adjustments you make are saved. Once
   updated, the access settings will immediately take effect.

- Use expiration dates to enhance security for shared links and communicate any permission changes to collaborators. To do this, open the sharing options window. Click **Anyone with the link can edit** (or a similar option depending on your needs). Enable the **Set expiration date** toggle. Choose the desired expiration date from the calendar. Click Apply to confirm the changes.

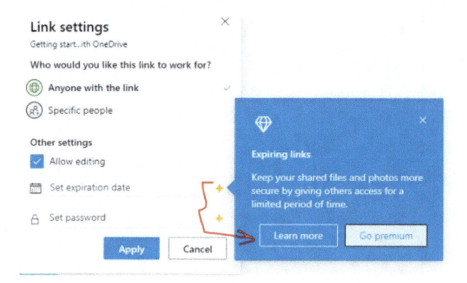

Password Protection

Password Protection: Add a password to access shared links for added security. You can input passwords to specific files and share the password with any collaborator that you want to have access.

How To Enable Notifications for Changes Made by Collaborators

- Click on **Share** (web interface) or **Manage Access** (desktop app).
- Ensure the file/folder is shared with collaborators by entering their email addresses or sharing a link.
- For the Web Interface, Click the gear icon (⚙) at the top right of the OneDrive page. Select **OneDrive Settings** from the dropdown. For the Desktop App, Right-click on the **OneDrive icon** in the system tray (bottom right of your screen). Click **Settings**, then navigate to the **Account** or **Notifications** tab.
- Enable the option for **Email notifications** or **Push notifications** (depending on your preference). On the web: Look for options like "Someone edits a file I shared." On mobile or desktop: Ensure app notifications are enabled through your device's settings.

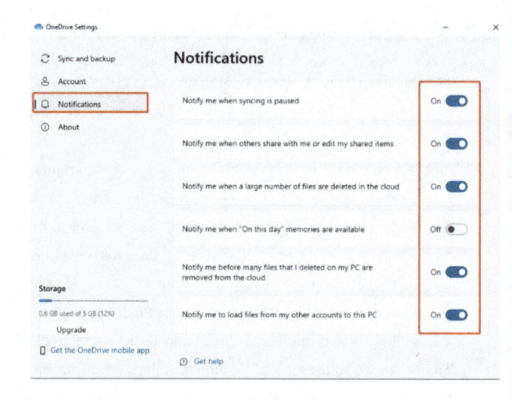

Sharing Large Files

- Compress files into ZIP archives if needed.
- Send links instead of attachments for very large files.

Practical Scenarios

Scenario 1: Collaboration on Team Project

- Share the document. Set editing permissions for members of the team.

- Use comments. Ask your team members to use comments to provide feedback.
- Monitor the progress of the project by checking the activity log to stay updated.

Scenario 2: Sharing Photos with Family

- Create a folder. Move your photos into the folder. Share the folder with family members. Allow a view-only access. Remember when we discussed about permissions right?
- Enable offline access for easy viewing.

Scenario 3: Collaborating on a Presentation

- Share your presentation with your colleagues. Allow editing for your colleague, or not. It depends on what you want.
- Use comments to provide suggestions directly in the file.

Scenario 4: Managing a Shared Team Folder

- Organize the folder using subfolders for different teams or tasks.
- Set permissions for each collaborator for each subfolder or task. Review the permissions periodically.

CHAPTER FIVE

ONEDRIVE FOR WORK AND SCHOOL

O neDrive can be an indispensable asset for both professional and educational environments. Whether you are managing a complex work project, collaborating on an academic research paper, or organizing class materials, OneDrive offers features designed to elevate your productivity and simplify your workflow. By mastering OneDrive, you can unlock a seamless, efficient approach to both work and school tasks.

OneDrive for Work

What you need is called OneDrive for Business. It is specifically engineered to meet the demands of professionals and organizations. This powerful tool integrates effortlessly with the entire suite of Microsoft 365 applications, providing a secure and collaborative platform for managing documents, files, and projects.

How to Setup OneDrive for Business

3. If you already have a Microsoft 365 subscription, you are ready to start using OneDrive for Business. Simply visit the OneDrive for

Business website or access it through the OneDrive app on your desktop for seamless integration.

4. Download and install the OneDrive sync client tailored for your operating system. This will synchronize your local files with OneDrive for Business, allowing for easier file management across devices.

5. Once installed, you can customize your sync settings to specify which folders and files you want to synchronize, ensuring you have access to the right documents at all times.

Organizing Work Files

- Establish a Folder Structure by creating a logical folder hierarchy. It is key to staying organized. For instance, organize your files by project, department, or client. This way, finding the right document becomes effortless.

- Use Naming Conventions. Implement consistent naming conventions for files and folders. A clear, standardized naming system will streamline file retrieval and management.

- Leverage Metadata and Tags. Enhance the organization of your files by adding metadata and tags. This extra layer of context will help quick searches and facilitate quick access. For example, a photographer might tag images by type—such as "nature," "office," or "dog"—making it easier to locate specific categories of photos in large collections.

Sharing and Collaboration on Work Documents

- Use OneDrive's **share** feature to provide access to documents. You can control permissions by selecting "Can Edit" or "Can View," depending on the level of access you wish to grant.
- Collaborate in real time. OneDrive allows multiple users to work on Word, Excel, or PowerPoint documents simultaneously. With live updates, changes are synchronized in real-time, ensuring all the collaborators are working on the most current version of the document.
- Use version history. You can track revisions and changes with OneDrive's version history. This feature lets you restore previous versions if needed, maintaining full control over your document's lifecycle.

Manage Permissions and Access

- Regularly assess who has access to your files. Permissions can be adjusted at any time to ensure that only authorized users have the ability to view or edit sensitive content.

- For added security, set expiration dates on shared links. This will automatically revoke access to the document after a predetermined time, reducing the risk of unauthorized access.
- Keep track of who has accessed or modified your files using the activity feed. This feature helps you monitor progress and ensures that your documents are being used appropriately.

Integrating OneDrive with Microsoft 365 Apps

Microsoft Teams Integration

1. Sign In to Microsoft Teams

   - Open the Microsoft Teams application or navigate to Microsoft Teams in your browser.
   - Sign in with your Microsoft account credentials.

2. Open or Create a Team

   - Navigate to the **Teams** section in the left-hand sidebar.
   - Select an existing team or click **Join or Create a Team** at the bottom to create a new one.
   - If creating a new team:
     - Click **Create Team**.
     - Choose a template (e.g., "From scratch").

- Name your team and adjust privacy settings (Public or Private).
- Click **Create**.

3. Access the Files Tab

   1. Select the team or channel where you want to integrate OneDrive.
   2. At the top of the channel, click the **Files** tab.

4. Add Cloud Storage (OneDrive)

   1. In the **Files** tab, click the **Add cloud storage** button (or the "+" icon).
   2. Select **OneDrive** from the list of available cloud storage options.
   3. You may be prompted to sign in to your Microsoft account if you're not already signed in.

5. Configure OneDrive Access

   1. Once signed in, OneDrive will integrate with the selected channel.
   2. You can now:
      - View your OneDrive files directly within Teams.
      - Upload new files or folders to OneDrive from Teams.

- Share files with team members.

6. Share OneDrive Files in Chats

1. Go to the **Chat** section in Teams.
2. Open an existing chat or start a new one.
3. Click the **Attach (paperclip)** icon below the message box.
4. Select **OneDrive**.
5. Browse and select the file you want to share, then click **Share**.

7. Collaborate on OneDrive Files in Teams

1. Open a shared OneDrive file in Teams.
2. Collaborate in real-time by editing the document using Microsoft Office apps (Word, Excel, or PowerPoint).
3. Changes are saved automatically, and team members can see updates instantly.

8. Adjust Permissions

When sharing files, ensure the correct permissions are set for team members:

- Click the **three dots (⋯)** next to a file in the **Files** tab.
- Select **Manage access**.

- Adjust permissions (e.g., "View" or "Edit") as necessary.

9. Use OneDrive in the Teams Mobile App (Optional)

   1. Open the Microsoft Teams app on your mobile device.
   2. Navigate to **Files** at the bottom of the screen.
   3. Select **OneDrive** to access and manage your OneDrive files directly from your phone.

10. Monitor Activity and Usage

    1. Use the **Activity Feed** in Teams to track changes to shared OneDrive files.
    2. Use OneDrive's version history to revert to previous versions if needed.

SharePoint Integration

1. Sign in to your **Microsoft 365** account through your web browser.
2. Navigate to **SharePoint** from the app launcher (often represented by a grid or tiles icon).
3. Access the site containing the files you wish to sync.

4. Locate the **Document Library** by clicking on the appropriate section or folder.

5. Within the SharePoint document library, locate and click the **Sync** button (typically found on the toolbar near the top of the page).

6. If prompted, allow the system to open your OneDrive app. This will start the synchronization process.

7. Follow any additional prompts to confirm the integration. You may need to sign in to your OneDrive for Business account if not already logged in.

8. Once synced, your SharePoint files will appear under a dedicated folder in your OneDrive directory: On Desktop: Open your File Explorer (Windows) or Finder (Mac), then locate the folder under the OneDrive section. On Mobile: Use the OneDrive app to view and manage synced SharePoint files.

9. To customize the Sync Settings, Open the OneDrive App settings on your device. Navigate to the **Account or Preferences** section. Adjust which SharePoint libraries or folders you want to sync to optimize storage and bandwidth usage.

You can open and edit OneDrive files directly from Office apps such as Word, Excel, and PowerPoint. Your changes are saved in OneDrive automatically, ensuring your files are always up to date across devices.

OneDrive for School

What you need is called OneDrive for Education. It mirrors the functionality of OneDrive for Business, but it is tailored specifically for students and educators. As part of Microsoft 365 Education, it provides powerful tools for managing coursework, collaborating on group assignments, and more.

How to Setup OneDrive for Education

- Students and educators with a Microsoft 365 Education subscription can access OneDrive for Education through the dedicated website or by installing the OneDrive app.
- After installing the OneDrive sync client, customize the settings to select which files and folders to synchronize between your device and OneDrive, ensuring access to everything you need.
- Set up folders for each subject or project, keeping your academic work well-organized. Be sure to apply consistent naming conventions to stay on top of your assignments and materials.

Using OneDrive for Academic Collaboration

- Share documents and folders with classmates or group members, and control permissions to allow them to view or edit the content.

- Take advantage of OneDrive's co-authoring features to collaborate on documents, presentations, and more. This ensures that every team member can contribute simultaneously, making teamwork more efficient.

- OneDrive allows you to access your school materials from any device, whether you're in class, at home, or on the go. This ensures that you can continue your work wherever you are.

Managing and Sharing Academic Content

- Easily share assignments, research, and notes with both teachers and peers. The sharing options give you full control over who can view or edit your files.

- Use OneDrive alongside Office 365 apps like Word, Excel, and PowerPoint to enhance your workflow. Collaborate directly within these applications for a more streamlined experience.

- With OneDrive, you can enable offline access for important files, allowing you to work on your projects even without an internet connection. Once online again, your changes will sync automatically.

Practical Scenario

Scenario 1: Collaborative Research Paper.

Let's assume that you and your classmates are working on a research paper and need to share documents, organize research materials, and track revisions.

- Share the document with your classmates, allowing them to edit and contribute.
- Store research articles, notes, and data in a shared folder for easy access and organization.
- Use OneDrive's version history feature to track changes and preserve the integrity of the paper.

Scenario 2: Managing Class materials.

Let us assume that you are a teacher, and you need to organize and share class materials with your students.

- Set up folders for each subject or unit, storing class materials and assignments in each folder.
- Share the folders with students, giving them access to class resources and assignments.
- Use OneDrive to manage student assignments, providing feedback and keeping track of submissions.

CHAPTER SIX

SECURING YOUR FILES ON ONEDRIVE

S afeguarding your files from unauthorized access and potential loss is paramount. OneDrive offers a range of powerful tools to keep your data secure. We will look into OneDrive's built-in security features, walk you through enabling two-factor authentication, and explain how to manage file versions. The real-life case study demonstrating how to keep both personal and work files safe will help give practical perspective.

What is OneDrive Security Features?

OneDrive has multiple layers of security to help you protect your files from both external threats and accidental loss. Let's check out some of the key security features:

Data Encryption

This is how OneDrive ensures safety of your files. It employs encryption both when your files are in transit and when they are stored on the cloud.

- Encryption in Transit: All data transferred between your device and OneDrive's servers is encrypted with TLS (Transport Layer Security), which ensures that your files remain secure as they travel over the internet, making it difficult for unauthorized parties to intercept or access them.
- Encryption at Rest: Once your files are stored on OneDrive's servers, they are encrypted using AES-256 (Advanced Encryption Standard with a 256-bit key). This is one of the most secure encryption standards available, designed to prevent unauthorized access even if someone were to gain physical access to the storage servers.

This might sound too technical. Thankfully you don't have to understand what they mean. All you need to know is that OneDrive has a system in place that ensures that your files are safe and remain safe.

Access Controls

OneDrive allows you to manage who has access to your files and what they can do with them. You therefore have the power to maintain control over your data:

- File and Folder Permissions: You can define specific permissions for individual files or entire folders, giving you flexibility to control access. Options include "Can view," "Can edit," and "Can share," enabling you to decide whether others can only view your documents or modify them.

- Sharing Links: When sharing files, OneDrive allows you to generate secure links with customizable permissions. You can set expiration dates and password-protect these links, adding an extra layer of protection.

File Activity Monitoring

OneDrive keeps track of who accesses or modifies your files, so you can stay on top of any changes:

- Activity Feed: With this feature, you get to see a history of interactions with your files, such as who accessed them and what changes were made. It's a great way to monitor collaboration and detect any unexpected alterations.

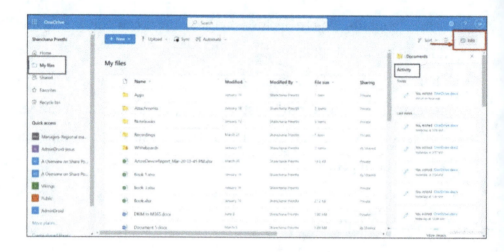

- **Notifications:** You can set up alerts to be notified whenever changes are made to files you share. This feature helps you stay informed about critical updates and prevents any surprises.

Ransomware Detection and Recovery

OneDrive offers features to help you combat the threats of ransomware attacks. These attacks are becoming increasingly common.

- **Ransomware Detection:** OneDrive actively scans for unusual behavior that may signal a ransomware attack. You'll be notified immediately if OneDrive detects encrypted files or other signs of an attack.

- File Recovery: OneDrive's file recovery tool allows you to restore your files to a prior version if they are corrupted by ransomware or other types of data loss.

To set up your backup, simply open OneDrive settings by clicking the cloud icon in your notification area. From there, you can manage your backup settings and enable automatic backups for added security.

How to Enable Two-Factor Authentication

Two-factor authentication (2FA) adds an extra layer of protection to your OneDrive account by requiring a second form of verification in addition to your password. This makes it much harder for attackers to gain access to your account, even if they manage to get your password.

- Go to the **Microsoft Account Security** page at account.microsoft.com and sign in with your credentials.

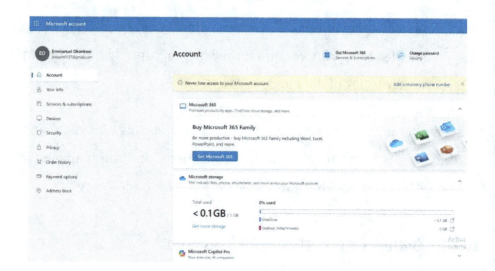

- Once logged in, navigate to **Security Settings** by clicking on the "Security" tab in the menu.

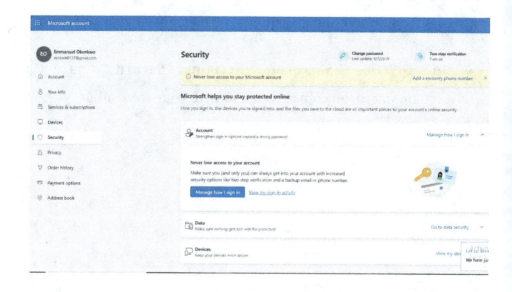

- Select **Two-Step Verification** under the **Advanced Security Options** section.

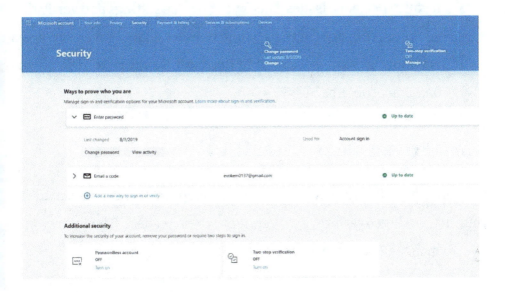

- Follow the instructions in the setup wizard, which will guide you through verifying your identity with a security code sent to your email or phone.
- Choose your preferred method of verification: through either text messages, authentication app, or via email.
- Once you've selected your preferred verification method and entered the verification code, your two-factor authentication will be activated.
- Generate backup codes: In case you lose access to your primary verification method, create backup codes.

- Store backup codes safely: Keep these codes in a secure place where only you can access them, such as a password manager.
- If you experience issues, check your device settings and verify that your authentication app or phone number is configured correctly.
- For more assistance, contact **Microsoft Support** to resolve any ongoing problems.

How to Recover Old Versions of Files

Version history in OneDrive allows you to keep track of changes made to your files and recover previous versions when needed. The following is how to manage and restore versions:

- Sign in to **OneDrive** and locate the file you wish to restore.
- Right-click on the file (or click the ellipsis next to it) and select **Version History** to view all previous versions.

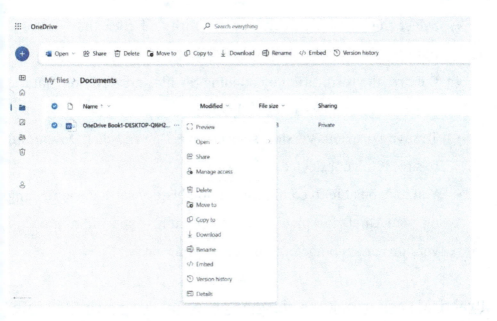

- Browse through the list of file versions, which includes the date, time, and author of each version.

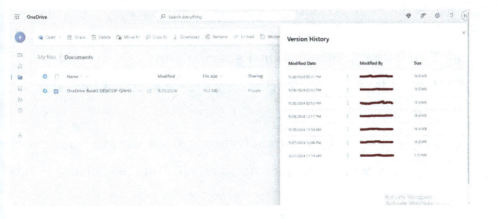

- You can preview any previous version before deciding to restore it.

- Select the version you want to restore and click the "Restore" button.
- Confirm the restoration by opening the file and verifying that the previous version is successfully restored.
- To save a previous version, select the version and click **Download** to save it to your device.
- You may be able to configure version history settings depending on your OneDrive plan, such as retaining a specific number of versions or keeping versions for a set period.

Practical Scenario: Keeping your personal and work files safe

Rachael is a marketing professional who uses OneDrive to manage both her personal and work files. Her experience in securing these files showcases the value of OneDrive's security features:

- Two-Factor Authentication: Rachael enabled 2FA, using Microsoft Authenticator to ensure that only she could access her OneDrive account.
- File Permissions: She carefully managed file access, sharing work files only with colleagues and personal files with close family members.

- Version History: When her team accidentally overwrote important marketing content, Rachael used version history to restore the previous draft, saving hours of work.
- Ransomware Recovery: Rachael's account was flagged for suspicious activity during a ransomware attack. Thanks to OneDrive's file recovery, she was able to restore her files and prevent data loss.

Summary of How to Secure Your Files on OneDrive

- Use Strong Passwords: Create unique and complex passwords for your Microsoft account.
- Enable Two-Factor Authentication: Always turn on 2FA for extra security.
- Manage Permissions: Regularly review who has access to your files and adjust permissions as necessary.
- Monitor Activity: Stay aware of who is accessing your files with activity logs and notifications.
- Use Encryption: Ensure all sensitive data is encrypted both in transit and at rest.
- Back Up Important Files: Regular backups to OneDrive ensure data integrity and recovery.
- Stay Informed: Keep up with OneDrive's latest security updates to stay ahead of potential threats.

CHAPTER SEVEN

MANAGING STORAGE SPACE

I n this chapter, you will be guided on how you can manage your storage space on OneDrive. You'll learn how to check your storage usage, get tips for freeing up space, evaluate if upgrading to more storage is worth it, and perform a final checkpoint to ensure your storage is optimized.

How to Check Your Storage Usage

Monitoring your storage usage is crucial to avoid running out of space. Here's how to check your OneDrive storage usage:

- Start by signing into your OneDrive account on your computer or mobile device.
- Navigate to the OneDrive web interface or open the OneDrive desktop app.
- On the web interface, click your profile picture or the gear icon (⚙) in the top-right corner. Select "Options" or "Settings" from the dropdown menu.

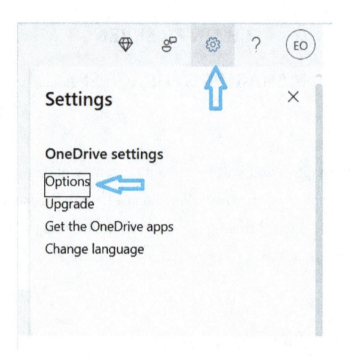

- Under "Manage Storage" view your current usage.

Tips for Freeing Up Space

- Delete unnecessary files: Review your folders for files or documents that are no longer needed, like outdated ones or duplicates. Select and delete unneeded files or move them to the Recycle Bin. To free up space completely, don't forget to empty the Recycle Bin.
- Organize and archive files: For files that you rarely need but want to keep, consider compressing them into ZIP archives to reduce

size. Move archived files to a different location in OneDrive or external storage.

- Use OneDrive's **Files On Demand**: This feature lets you see all your files in File Explorer without taking up local storage. Files are only downloaded when accessed. To enable it, right-click the OneDrive icon in your taskbar, and select "Settings."

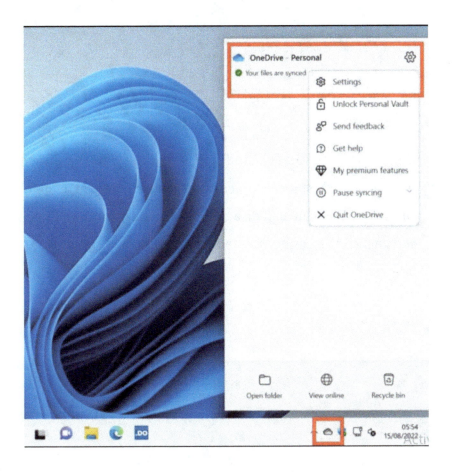

In the "Sync and Backup" section. Click on "Advanced Settings."

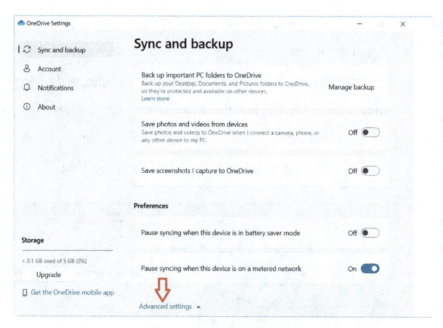

Under the "Files On-Demand" tab, select the "Free up disk space" option to remove local copies of files but keep them available in OneDrive. You can also disable Files-On-Demand by going to settings and selecting "Download All Files."

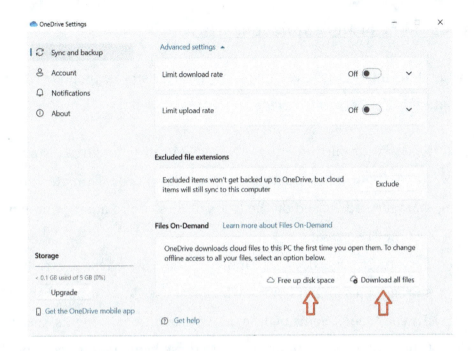

- Delete old versions of files: Use OneDrive's version history to review and delete older versions of files that you no longer need. See Chapter 6 for more details on using this feature. Periodically remove outdated versions to free up space while retaining the most recent versions.

- Remove shared files: Check shared files and revoke access to those you no longer need to share. In OneDrive, go to the "Shared" section to view and manage your shared files.

- Optimize storage in the OneDrive app: Adjust your OneDrive desktop app settings to sync only the files and folders you need. Enable selective sync to limit the folders that sync to your device, conserving local storage.

Is Upgrading to More Storage Worth It?

If you often run out of space, upgrading to more storage may be worth considering. Here's how to decide:

- Assess Your Current Storage Needs: Review your current storage to see how much additional space you need. Estimate future storage needs based on the types of files you're adding and how fast they're growing.

- Explore Storage Upgrade Options: OneDrive offers a variety of storage plans for personal and business use. Find the one that best fits your needs. Some plans come with additional benefits, such as Office 365 subscriptions. Evaluate these benefits to determine if they add value.

- Evaluate the Cost-Benefit Ratio: Consider the cost of upgrading and weigh it against benefits like increased productivity and extra storage. Make sure the upgrade fits your budget. If it does, the added space can bring peace of mind.

- Make an Informed Decision: Decide if a short-term or long-term plan is more appropriate. If you're unsure, continue monitoring your storage to see if additional space becomes necessary.

- Implement the Upgrade: Follow the instructions provided by OneDrive to select and pay for your new storage plan. After upgrading, apply the earlier tips to manage your new space effectively.

CHAPTER EIGHT

ADVANCED FEATURES AND INTEGRATIONS

This chapter introduces OneDrive's advanced features and integrations, which can enhance productivity and streamline workflows. We'll cover on a basic level integration with other cloud services and apps, provide a real-world example of workflow optimization, and share expert tips for maximizing OneDrive efficiency.

Integrating OneDrive with Third-Party Apps

1. Cloud Storage Aggregators

Integrating OneDrive with Zapier to Automate Workflow

Zapier is an automation platform that connects apps and services without requiring coding knowledge. Using Zapier, you can automate workflows, known as **Zaps**, that trigger actions in OneDrive when specific events occur in other apps—or vice versa.

- Go to Zapier's website. Click **Sign Up** and follow the steps to create an account.
- Visit the Zapier dashboard after signing up or logging in.

- In Zapier, click on your profile icon in the top-right corner and select **Connected Accounts**.
- Click **Connect a New Account**, search for **OneDrive**, and click on it.
- A pop-up window will appear asking for your Microsoft login credentials. Enter them and grant Zapier access to your OneDrive account.
- Decide what automation you want to create. Here are some examples:
  - Save Gmail attachments to a OneDrive folder.
  - Upload new files from Dropbox to OneDrive.
  - Notify you via Slack when a file is added to a specific OneDrive folder.
- Go to the Zap Editor: In the Zapier dashboard, click **Create Zap**.
- Set Up the Trigger: A trigger is an event that starts the workflow. Choose the app that will act as the trigger. For example: If you want to save Gmail attachments to OneDrive, select **Gmail**.
- Select the event that will trigger the workflow, such as **New Attachment**.
- Follow the prompts to log in to the app and test the trigger.
- Set Up the Action: An action is what happens after the trigger. Select **OneDrive** as the action app.

- Choose the specific action to perform, such as **Upload File** or **Create Folder**.

- Connect your OneDrive account if not already done.

- Customize the Action: Specify details for the action, such as the folder in OneDrive where files should be uploaded.

- Use data from the trigger app (e.g., Gmail attachment file names) to customize the workflow.

- Test Your Zap: Zapier allows you to test the trigger and action to ensure they work as intended. Run the test and verify the outcome by checking OneDrive for the expected results.

- Once the test is successful, Click **Turn On Zap** to activate it. Your automation will now run whenever the trigger event occurs.

Transfer files seamlessly between OneDrive and Dropbox

OneDrive and Dropbox are separate platforms without native, direct file transfer features. You can use download-upload methods or third-party tools for a smoother experience. Verify that you have sufficient storage space in Dropbox to accommodate the files being transferred from OneDrive.

- Log in to your **Microsoft OneDrive** account at onedrive.com. Log in to your **Dropbox** account at dropbox.com.

- Organize the files or folders you want to transfer by grouping them logically in OneDrive.

- Check the file sizes and total storage required to ensure it aligns with Dropbox's available space.

- Rename files or folders (if needed) to maintain clarity in Dropbox.

- Navigate to your files on the **OneDrive** web interface.

- Select the desired files or folders. Use **Ctrl + Click** (Windows) or **Cmd + Click** (Mac) to select multiple items.

- Click the **Download** button on the top toolbar.

- The files will be downloaded as individual items or as a compressed (ZIP) file, depending on the selection.

- Locate the downloaded files in your computer's **Downloads** folder or the directory you specified.

- Locate the downloaded files in your computer's **Downloads** folder or the directory you specified. Place the extracted files in an easily accessible location on your computer.

- Open your **Dropbox** account in a web browser or use the **Dropbox desktop app**.

- Navigate to the location where you want to store the files.

- Click the **Upload** button and select the files or folders you downloaded from OneDrive. If using the web interface, drag and drop files directly into the browser window as an alternative.

- Monitor the upload progress to ensure all files are transferred successfully.
- After the upload completes, check your Dropbox account to confirm that all files have been transferred correctly.
- Open a few files to ensure their integrity and accessibility.
- Compare the files in Dropbox with the originals in OneDrive to confirm no data is missing.
- Organize files in Dropbox to match your original OneDrive structure.

2. Project Management Tools

Linking OneDrive with Trello

- Log in to Trello and navigate to the board where you want to integrate files. Ensure you have appropriate access to add attachments or integrations.
- Trello's Power-Ups extend its functionality, including integration with OneDrive.
- To enable Trello's Power-Ups, Open the Trello board where you want to attach files.
- Click on the **Power-Ups** button, typically located in the board menu on the right.
- Search for **OneDrive** in the Power-Up directory.

- Select OneDrive and click **Add** or **Enable**.

- Once the OneDrive Power-Up is enabled, click on it within the board.

- Follow the prompts to sign in to your Microsoft account.

- Grant Trello permission to access your OneDrive files. This step ensures seamless sharing between the two platforms.

- Now that the integration is set up, you can attach OneDrive files to Trello cards: Open the card where you want to add a file.

- Click on the **Attach File** or **OneDrive** button within the card options.

- Browse your OneDrive files and select the document you want to link.

- Confirm the attachment, and it will appear on the Trello card for all members to access.

- To ensure seamless collaboration: **Label Cards:** Use labels to indicate the type of file or its purpose. **Add Comments:** Provide context about the attached file by adding comments to the card. **Update Files:** If a file is modified in OneDrive, the updated version will reflect in Trello, provided the link remains active.

- Open the Trello card containing the attached OneDrive file.

- Click the file link to open it directly in OneDrive, where you can view, edit, or download it.

Linking OneDrive with Asana

Asana and Microsoft OneDrive are both widely used tools that support effective task management and cloud-based file storage. Integrating these platforms allows you to attach OneDrive files directly to tasks in Asana, streamlining workflows and enhancing team collaboration.

To begin, make sure you have the following: An active **Microsoft 365** account with access to OneDrive, An account with **Asana** (free or premium versions both support file attachments), and Permissions to share files stored in OneDrive.

- Log In to Both Platforms
- Open Asana and navigate to your **Apps** menu. This can usually be found by clicking your profile picture or accessing the **Admin Console**.
- Look for the **OneDrive Integration** under the list of available apps or use the search bar to find it quickly.
- Click on **Install or Connect** and follow the on-screen prompts to link OneDrive to your Asana workspace.
- Open a Task in Asana: Navigate to the project and task to which you want to attach a file.
- Click on the Paperclip Icon: Locate the attachment option within the task details pane.

- Choose OneDrive as the Source: In the file picker dialog box, select **OneDrive** as the source for your file attachment. If prompted, log in to your Microsoft account to authenticate the connection.

- Select a File: Browse your OneDrive folders, select the desired file, and click **Attach**. The file will now be linked to the task for all collaborators to access.

- Adjust Sharing Settings in OneDrive: Make sure the attached file has the appropriate sharing permissions. Files linked in Asana are shared using OneDrive's sharing settings.

- Set Access Levels: Choose whether collaborators can view, edit, or comment on the file. This ensures seamless collaboration while maintaining data security.

- Once linked, OneDrive files can be accessed directly from Asana: Open the task containing the attachment.

- Click on the file link to view or edit it in OneDrive.

- Changes made to the file will automatically sync to OneDrive and remain up to date in Asana.

3. Backup Tools

Linking OneDrive with Backblaze

Microsoft OneDrive and Backblaze are excellent tools for cloud storage and backup. While there isn't a direct integration between the two, you can establish a workflow to ensure that your OneDrive files are backed up to Backblaze.

It's important to recognize the purpose of linking OneDrive with Backblaze: Provides an additional layer of security for your critical files. It ensures data recovery in case OneDrive encounters an issue. It combines the best features of file syncing (OneDrive) and cloud backups (Backblaze).

- Log in to OneDrive and Backblaze accounts. Go to the Backblaze website and create an account if you don't already have one. Download and install the Backblaze backup client for your operating system.
- Locate the **OneDrive folder** on your computer where all your synced files are stored. On Windows: It's typically found in C:\Users\<YourName>\OneDrive. On Mac: It's usually in the ~/OneDrive directory.
- Confirm that this folder contains all the files you want to back up.
- Open the Backblaze app and navigate to the **Backup Settings** section.
- Select the **Files to Backup** option. By default, Backblaze automatically backs up all user files except for system files and certain exclusions.

- Ensure that the OneDrive folder is included in the list of directories to back up. If it isn't: Click **Add Folder** or a similar option in the Backblaze interface. Browse and select the OneDrive folder.
- Save your changes to apply the updated backup configuration.
- Start the backup process by clicking the **Backup Now** button in Backblaze. Depending on the size of your OneDrive folder and your internet speed, this initial backup may take some time.
- Monitor the progress using the Backblaze app dashboard, which provides detailed information about upload speed and files being backed up.
- Once the backup is complete, log in to your Backblaze account on their website.
- Navigate to the **Restore Files** section to ensure your OneDrive files are listed and accessible.
- Verify that the folder structure in Backblaze matches your OneDrive folder.
- Backblaze is designed to automatically back up changes in real time. Ensure the following settings are enabled: **Continuous Backup:** This ensures that any new or modified files in your OneDrive folder are automatically backed up to Backblaze. **Exclude Unnecessary Files:** Review and adjust Backblaze's exclusions list to prevent unwanted files from being backed up.

Practical Scenario

This example illustrates how a marketing team used OneDrive integrations to optimize workflow, improve collaboration, and boost productivity.

Background

A marketing team struggled with disorganized files across multiple tools. They sought a solution to improve file management and streamline workflow.

Solution

1. Microsoft Office Integration
   - Centralized Document Storage: By saving all marketing documents to OneDrive, team members could access and edit the latest versions, reducing version control issues.
   - Real-Time Collaboration: Office applications integrated with OneDrive allowed real-time editing, speeding up collaboration.
2. Project Management Integration
   - Attaching Files to Trello: By linking OneDrive to Trello, the team attached relevant files to tasks, enhancing organization.

- Automating Task Updates: Automated workflows ensured Trello cards reflected recent OneDrive changes, improving project oversight.

3. Automating File Transfers

- Automating File Syncs: Zapier automated file transfers between OneDrive and other platforms, simplifying file handling.
- Centralized Asset Management: Marketing assets were synced across platforms, ensuring easy access to updated creative files.

Results

- Improved Collaboration: Real-time document access and organized task management allowed faster decision-making.
- Enhanced Efficiency: Reduced manual work, centralized storage, and automated backups saved time and protected assets.

Tips for Maximizing OneDrive Efficiency

For users seeking to leverage OneDrive's full potential, here are expert tips to boost productivity:

1. Master Keyboard Shortcuts

- Use Keyboard Shortcuts: Learn shortcuts like *Ctrl + Shift + N* (new folder) or *Ctrl + A* (select all) for faster navigation.
- Customize Shortcuts: Adjust shortcut settings to streamline frequent tasks.

2. Utilize Advanced Search Features
   - Search Filters: Apply filters like file type or date to quickly find files.
   - Search Operators: Use operators (AND, OR, NOT) to refine search results for specific files.

3. Automate Routine Tasks
   - Set Up Automations: With Power Automate, save email attachments to OneDrive or automatically move files between folders.
   - Create Custom Workflows: Design custom flows that integrate with OneDrive for recurring tasks.

4. Organize with Metadata
   - Apply Metadata and Tags: Classify files by applying metadata and tags to aid in searching and organizing.
   - Filter with Metadata: Find files quickly by filtering them based on their metadata.

5. Monitor and Manage Storage
   - Regularly Check Storage: Use storage tips (see Chapter 7) to manage your available space.

- Optimize Settings: Adjust sync settings to control local storage usage.

6. Explore the OneDrive API

   - Develop Custom Integrations: If you're technically inclined, use the OneDrive API for custom integrations that enhance file management.
   - Automate Complex Workflows: Build tailored workflows that connect OneDrive with other services based on your unique needs.

7. Stay Updated with New Features

   - Follow Updates: Keep up with new OneDrive releases and features.
   - Experiment with Tools: Test new tools and features as they become available to improve your OneDrive experience.

CHAPTER NINE

HOW TO TROUBLESHOOT ISSUES

How to Resolve Syncing Issues

Syncing issues can prevent files from updating across your devices. Here's a guide to troubleshoot and resolve these problems:

1. Check OneDrive Status

- Verify Sync Status: Open the OneDrive app by clicking on the cloud icon in your system tray (Windows) or menu bar (macOS). A green checkmark indicates files are synced; a blue spinning icon shows syncing in progress.
- Look for Error Messages: Notifications may alert you to any sync issues. Click on the OneDrive icon to view error messages and suggested solutions.

2. Troubleshoot Common Syncing Issues

- Check Internet Connection: Verify your internet connectivity, as a stable connection is essential for syncing.

- Restart OneDrive and Your Computer: Restarting OneDrive or your device can often resolve underlying system issues.
- Check File Size and Type: OneDrive has a 100 GB file size limit (depending on subscription) and supports specific file types.
- Resolve Conflicts: Sync conflicts may result in duplicate files. Review and delete or merge conflicting files as needed.

How to Deal with File Upload Failures

File upload issues can disrupt your workflow. Use these steps to troubleshoot:

1. Verify File and Folder Names

- Avoid Special Characters: Remove unsupported characters such as /, :, *, ?, ", <, >, | from file names.
- Check Name Length: OneDrive has a 400-character limit for file paths. Shorten names if necessary.

2. Check File Size and Type

- Review File Size Limits: Files over the limit may need to be split or compressed.
- Verify Supported Formats: Confirm that files are in supported formats, converting them if needed.

3. Clear Upload Cache

- Clear Cache: Free up space by right-clicking on your OneDrive folder and selecting "Free up space."
- Restart OneDrive: Restarting can help resolve temporary issues with uploads.

How to Solve Access Issues and Missing Files

Having trouble accessing your files or locating missing items? Follow these steps:

1. Verify File Location

- Search for Files: Use OneDrive's search function to locate misplaced files.
- Review Shared Files: Verify that shared folders are still accessible.

2. Check Account and Permissions

- Confirm Account Access: Ensure you're logged into the correct OneDrive account.
- Manage Sharing Permissions: Check file sharing settings, and confirm that sharing links are active.

3. Resolve Sync Issues

- Force a Sync: Pause and then resume syncing by selecting "Help and settings" on OneDrive's popup menu.
- Restart OneDrive: Restarting OneDrive or your computer can resolve persistent sync problems.

4. Check for Known Issues

- Visit OneDrive Status Page: Microsoft's OneDrive status page can alert you to any known issues or outages affecting services.

To Check If Your Files Are Running Smoothly

Take a moment to evaluate your OneDrive setup and address any issues:

1. Review Sync Status: Confirm that all files are updated and available across devices.
2. Validate Uploads: Check that recent uploads are successful and accessible.
3. Assess Access and Permissions: Ensure access to all files and review sharing settings.
4. Check File Organization: Verify that your files and folders are well-organized.

5. Monitor Storage Usage: Keep track of OneDrive storage and free up space if necessary.

6. Test Offline Access: Ensure offline files are accessible and changes sync once reconnected.

INDEX